Touring
New Jersey's
Lighthouses

Mary Beth Temple
Photography by Patricia Wylupek

Schiffer
Publishing Ltd
4880 Lower Valley Road, Atglen, PA 19310 USA

Library of Congress Cataloging-in-Publication Data:

Temple, Mary Beth.
  Touring New Jersey's lighthouses / by Mary Beth Temple ;
photography by Patricia Wylupek.
      p. cm.
  ISBN 0-7643-2093-9 (pbk.)
  1. Lighthouses—New Jersey. I. Wylupek, Patricia. II. Title.
  VK1024.N5T46 2004
  387.1'55'09749—dc22

                         2004006277

Designed by John P. Cheek
Type set in Footlight MT Light/Aldine721 Lt BT
ISBN: 0-7643-2093-9
Printed in China

Published by Schiffer Publishing Ltd.
4880 Lower Valley Road
Atglen, PA 19310
Phone: (610) 593-1777; Fax: (610) 593-2002
E-mail: Info@schifferbooks.com

For the largest selection of fine reference books on this and related subjects,
please visit our web site at www.schifferbooks.com
We are always looking for people to write books on new and related subjects. If
you have an idea for a book please contact us at the above address.

This book may be purchased from the publisher.
Include $3.95 for shipping.
Please try your bookstore first.
You may write for a free catalog.

In Europe, Schiffer books are distributed by
Bushwood Books
6 Marksbury Ave.
Kew Gardens
Surrey TW9 4JF England
Phone: 44 (0) 20 8392-8585; Fax: 44 (0) 20 8392-9876
E-mail: info@bushwoodbooks.co.uk
Free postage in the U.K., Europe; air mail at cost.

Dedication

As always, I dedicate my work to my large and loving family – the McCabes in all their extensions, and my husband, John, and daughter, Katie. Now we have to find another excuse to go "down the shore!"

– MBT

This book is dedicated to my husband, William, my daughter, Jennifer, and her husband, Chris; my daughter Alicia and her husband, Robert, and their children, Ryan and Daniel, with much love.

– PAW

Acknowledgments

I would like to thank Tom Laverty, president of the New Jersey Lighthouse Society and a Resource Interpretive Specialist at the Navesink Lighthouse. He was a big help in checking facts and clarifying information. Thanks also to Al Smith, Tom Walker at Supawna Meadows, Beth Huch at Tuckerton Seaport, and Sara Cureton at Absecon Lighthouse for their assistance checking facts. Thanks to the terrific staff at the New York Public Libraries, 42nd Street and Madison Avenue locations, and the staff at Tenafly (New Jersey) Library for helping me find great books. And special thanks to John Temple, first copy editor of all of my work whether he likes it or not.

– MBT

I want to thank Tom Laverty, Elinore and Rich Veit from Absecon Lighthouse, Betty Mugnier and Steve Murray from Hereford Lighthouse, my friend Rich Chiemingo from Cape May Lighthouse, and finally my husband, William, for his infinite patience and love.

– PAW

Contents

Introduction

"Among the many works of man which prove the truth of the saying that 'knowledge is power,' we must not omit those solitary towers, often half buried in the surge, that convert hidden dangers into sources of safety, so that the sailor now steers for those very rocks which he formerly dreaded and took so much care to avoid."
Thomas Stevenson, 1881
Lighthouse Construction and Illumination

Much has been written about the "constant" or "unchanging" sea. But I think that such descriptions can cause us to underestimate the power of the ocean. More accurate would be "pounding" sea, "powerful" sea, "constant" not as in static, but as in unrelenting. In the battle of man against nature, the pounding waves still have the advantage – they toss our ships against the rocks with resulting loss of life and goods; they cause land to appear, then to disappear, changing the geography of the seacoast at their discretion. Their goal may take years to accomplish, but the waves are patient, they can wait, secure in the knowledge that ultimately they will triumph.

Lighthouses are landmarks in many ways – they represent the architectural styles and lifestyles of the people who built them. But they also are landmarks of man's struggle to carve out a secure place in the natural world. Lest we forget, even in today's high-tech world, we are still but tenants on the Earth, still vulnerable to forces of nature even though those forces are far removed from the way we live now. Technology cannot keep us safe should Mother Nature turn against us.

Cape May Lighthouse at dusk.

View of Cape May from the top of the Cape May Lighthouse.

Yet the ocean is as beautiful as it is dangerous. Standing on top of Sandy Hook Lighthouse and looking out to the ocean lets us know that Nature in all her glory is still out there, waiting to be appreciated. The view has changed, there is a great city where once there was a huddling village, but the look of the sea remains the same – constant, almost comforting with its pulsing waves. Here it is easy to think of those who stood in this spot before us, men and women who lived their lives over the last two centuries, who threw themselves bodily into the fight for survival, creating beacons of safety where none previously existed, and going out at great personal risk into the perilous sea to rescue potential victims and drag them to safety.

New Jersey's lighthouses hold a unique place in history – the oldest standing lighthouse in the country is in the Garden State, along with lighthouses that were home to other firsts. There were many lighthouses and lightships along Jersey's coast that no longer exist, and there are terrific books that describe their histories. This book focuses on the eleven lighthouses in New Jersey that you can visit today. Although some have limited visiting hours, all of the lighthouses mentioned in this book are accessible to the public via land. So put down this book, turn off your cell phones and your laptops, get out there and experience an important part of New Jersey's and the country's history. Ponder what life was like 150 years ago, think about the history these buildings have been a part of, imagine what they will witness in the future, and absorb your surroundings. You won't find a better way to witness the awesome beauty of the ocean anywhere else.

CHAPTER 1
A Very Brief
History of Lighthouses

Scholars have never been able to definitively establish where the very first lighthouse stood, but all agree its origins must have been when early cultures lit bonfires on the shore to guide sailors home. The oldest documented lighthouse structure was on Pharos, an island at the mouth of Alexandria Harbor, Egypt. One of the Seven Wonders of the Ancient World, the Pharos, as it came to be called, is believed to have been built around 300 B.C. While no original drawings exist, archeologists think that the tower stood more than 350 feet tall, making it the tallest structure in ancient times. Fire signaled ships by night, and during the day, ships were signaled by the use of a huge mirror to reflect the rays of the sun.

The Alexandria Lighthouse was most certainly a marvel of early engineering and it stood until the early fourteenth century. If this structure was the first lighthouse architecturally, it was also the first lighthouse linguistically. *Pharus* is the Latin word for lighthouse, and very early English usage called them *pharo*. The words for lighthouse are also similar in French, Italian, and Spanish. The early Romans built many lighthouses as well. Ostia, which was built around 50 B.C. is the earliest Roman lighthouse documented. It is estimated by some that there were at least thirty Roman lighthouses in operation by the Empire's decline in the fifth century A.D.

Here in the New World, it is generally agreed that the first lighthouse tower was Boston Light, built on Little Brewster Island (then called Beacon Island) at the entrance to Boston Harbor. Funds for its construction were authorized by the General Court of Massachusetts in 1715, and the tall (estimated to stand approximately 75 feet tall) stone tower was first lit on September 14, 1716. The original tower did not survive the rigors of the Revolutionary War. After various skirmishes for possession, all of which damaged the tower, the British Fleet blew the lighthouse up on its way out of Boston in 1776. Another structure was later built on this site, and is still in use today.

As years went by and navigational needs changed, so did the administration of the United States' lighthouses. The construction of early lighthouses was authorized by local governments and supported by shipping taxes. Lights were placed where they would be of most use to commercial fleets, not necessarily the most hazardous places to sail. Lighthouse construction was time consuming and expensive, and no colony wanted to pay for a lighthouse in someone else's territory in the interest of safety. These projects were originally undertaken as part of a harsh business climate, not out of any humanitarian desires. In placing early lighthouses, loss of life was not as important as loss of goods. It is no accident that early lighthouses were clustered near densely populated areas and commercial hubs.

In 1789, Congress passed an act that allowed the federal government to take responsibility for all aids to navigation. This responsibility bounced back and forth between the Treasury Department and the Commissioner of Revenue until 1820, when it came to rest with Stephen Pleasonton, fifth auditor of the Treasury. The Pleasonton years were marked by his firm control of the purse strings, as well as his complete disregard of the need for a cohesive lighthouse system. Hard-working though he may have been, Pleasonton, in his thirty-two years at the helm of America's lighthouses, favored economy over function. Although Congress sent out a naval inspection team in 1838 to compile an accurate condition report of how the lighthouse system worked, it wasn't until 1852 that Congress created the Lighthouse Board, a group of representatives from the Navy, the Army Corps of Engineers, and civilians with a scientific background.

The lighthouse system was finally controlled by people who could understand all the aspects of its purpose. There were vast improvements in the quality of the United States' aids to the navigation system during the Lighthouse Board years. Lights were placed where they were most needed by mariners, not where the coast was most densely populated, and standards for the quality of lights and equipment were established. In 1910, the Lighthouse Board was replaced by the Bureau of Lighthouses in an attempt to increase civilian input into the system, and to reduce levels of bureaucracy. One person was assigned as head of the bureau, instead of the nine who ran the board. In 1939, responsibility for all aids to navigation was transferred to the United States Coast Guard.

A Few Important Lighthouse Terms

As the lighthouse administration developed and became more efficient, so did lighthouse maintenance and equipment. One of the most important developments was the use of the *Fresnel lens*. Invented in 1822 in France by physicist Augustin Fresnel, these large, heavy constructions of thick glass prisms were a huge improvement to the quality and visibility of a lighthouse's light. Fresnel lenses were made in seven orders; the 1st order is the largest, while the 6th order is the smallest (there is a 3.5 order light, which brings the total to seven). Coastal lights used the larger orders, river lights the smaller ones. While inquiries about these lenses were made by Stephen Pleasonton early in his tenure, he was loath to commit the amount of money necessary to purchase and install them. Not only were Fresnel lenses expensive, they required a time-consuming adjustment when first installed that necessitated hiring skilled labor, and the first one was not in service in the United States until 1841. Captain (later Commodore) Matthew Perry brought the first lenses here from Paris to be installed in the Navesink Lighthouse. The Lighthouse Board saw to it that all United States lighthouses were fitted with Fresnel lenses as new towers were built and old equipment replaced. Many of New Jersey's lighthouses have Fresnel lenses either in their tower or an accompanying museum; they are beautiful to look at.

4th Order Fresnel lens on display at the Tuckerton Seaport.

A lighthouse's lamp helps sailors navigate at night and during times of poor visibility, but a lighthouse's physical appearance helps sailors navigate by day as well. Both the light and the lighthouse must have distinguishing features. If all lighthouses looked alike, a navigator could not tell what section of the coast he was passing, so the lighthouse would not serve its purpose well. To that end, each lighthouse has a different light characteristic, fixed or flashing, white or colored, with various orders of lenses. To be able to identify them during the day, lighthouses are painted different colors. The distinguishing appearance of a lighthouse is referred to as its *daymark*. In New Jersey, daymarks are especially important 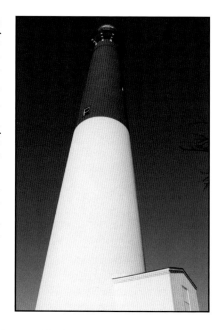 on the conical towers. It is easy in passing to distinguish the Sandy Hook tower from the fortress style Twin Lights, but not so easy to tell Absecon from her sister lights in Cape May and Barnegat without the aid of color.

Another point of reference is the tower's height. Throughout this book, I will refer to a lighthouse's *focal plane*. Focal plane is the distance from the center of the light source to sea level. Tower measurements can differ depending on where one starts and stops measuring, the beach conditions, or even the way the landscaping was done. The tower itself does not grow or shrink, but the measurement does. The focal plane measurement remains constant. This came to my attention when I noticed that several reference books refer to different tower heights for the same New Jersey lighthouse. It is interesting to note the difference between a lighthouse's focal plane and its tower height. The most obvious difference is at Twin Lights, where the 73 foot tower boasts a 246 foot focal plane.

The last terms I would like to define are *front* and *rear range lights*. Navigators passing the coastal lighthouses of New Jersey could see one light and judge their distance relative to it. But to navigate the Deleware Bay, mariners would tell their positions by using a set or *range* of two lights. One light in the range was taller than the other, and had a distinguishing feature. By looking at the relationship of the two lights to one another, sailors could determine whether or not they were sailing the channel properly. If the lighthouses did not line up in a certain way, course adjustments had to be made. One range light is not much use from a navigational standpoint without the other, but in some cases of historic lightouse towers, only one of a range is still standing. Finn's Point and Tinicum are each the rear range lights from their respective sets.

Above & Opposite page:
Contrasting daymarks, Absecon and Barnegat.

CHAPTER 2
Sandy Hook Lighthouse

Sandy Hook Lighthouse
Gateway National Recreation Area
Sandy Hook, New Jersey
732-872-5970

The Sandy Hook Lighthouse is the oldest standing lighthouse in the United States. It has run almost continuously since it was first lit in 1764 (it was doused on a few occasions during periods when the United States was at war) and is still active. The lighting equipment is maintained by the United States Coast Guard, while the building is in the Gateway National Recreation Area in Sandy Hook, and is maintained by the National Park Service. Tours and talks are presented by members of the New Jersey Lighthouse Society.

The United States was originally but a dream. The early colonists came to the New World to build this dream, but had to use materials from another place. There was no FedEx, no UPS, no Post Office with next-day guarantees and delivery confirmation, so the colonists relied on ships to bring not just luxuries, but also the necessities of a growing town – New York City! And after a wait of perhaps months, never exactly sure when your "ship would come in," you get the bad news – your long-awaited merchandise made the trip from Europe safely, but the ship was wrecked on that damnable sand bar that made the entry into New York Harbor so treacherous. From this climate, the idea for the Sandy Hook Lighthouse was born.

Sandy Hook is aptly named; it is a narrow strip of sandy land that protrudes into New York Harbor in a hook shape. Home to the Navesink Indians, the area had been touched upon by several explorers, most notably Henry Hudson, as early as 1609, but had not been not heavily settled by Europeans. Several explorers claimed the land for their native countries, as the Native American population looked on in bemusement.

In 1761, the New York Provincial Congress approved a lottery for the express purpose of raising funds for a lighthouse at Sandy Hook. Seven hundred fifty pounds were raised to purchase 4 acres of land from Robert and Esek Hartshorne. In 1762, Congress approved more lottery drawings which were held in 1763, the same year construction on the lighthouse finally began. At last, the New York Lighthouse (as it was then called) was lit on June 11, 1764. The light source was whale oil. The keeper's job was to keep the light burning: the forty-eight wicks trimmed, the oil supplied. Operating costs for the lighthouse were paid for by a duty imposed on all items shipped into New York Harbor.

The plans for the lighthouse tower were simple. The thick, stone building was an octagonal shaped tower, 103-feet tall, painted white. It was built by Isaac Conro, who also built a nearby house for the keeper. Originally constructed 500 feet from the ocean's reach, over the years the land has been built up by the sea, and the tower now stands approximately 1.5 miles from the surf. A stout circular staircase of 95 steps is used to reach the top of the tower, and there are large rectangular windows placed along the staircase. The window placement was more practical than decorative; the oils used to keep the lamps burning in the early days of lighthouses were not particularly efficient by today's standards, and generated a lot of smoke. Good ventilation was required to keep the wicks burning efficiently, and to prevent the poor keeper from choking to death while he was at work. The lamps had to be tended from sunset to sunrise, seven days a week, no matter what mood or state of health the keeper was in. The tower had a focal plane of 88 feet and originally showed a fixed light powered by forty-eight wicks burning whale oil in a regular glass lantern.

What was a great boon to the Colonies in 1764 became a potential liability to the emerging United States in 1774. With the British Fleet arriving to stamp out the burgeoning revolution, the same New York Provincial Congress that championed the building of the light just a few years before now ordered it dismantled so that it could not be used by the invaders to guide their entry into New York Harbor. In March of 1776, lighthouse supplies including eight copper lamps and four casks of whale oil were removed from the lighthouse by Colonial soldiers. Supported by a nearby frigate, British Loyalists managed to take control of the lighthouse, which they controlled for most of the Revolution. Colonial attempts to take it back included an hour-long barrage of cannon fire that did almost no damage to the well-built lighthouse. As soon as the Revolutionary War was over, the Sandy Hook Lighthouse was once again used for its original purpose, guiding ships headed into New York and preventing them from foundering on the sand bar.

Without the British to fight with, the governments of New York and New Jersey took to arguing with each other over ownership of and responsibility for the lighthouse; each state wanted control of the tonnage tax that was used to pay the lighthouse's maintenance expenses. The dispute ended when the Federal government assumed responsibility for the operation of all lighthouses in 1789.

In 1817, two beacons were built to aid the Sandy Hook light in its work, one to mark the bay and another to mark the seaside of the Hook. This was the first of several instances in the story of New Jersey lighthouses that the ever-changing geography of the Jersey shore had a direct effect on lighthouses and their locations. Both the East and West Beacons (as they were originally called) were replaced and relocated, as the grounds they were built on eroded and/or shifted. Although the West Beacon (renamed the South Beacon after a move) was dismantled in the 1920s when it became obsolete, the East Beacon shines on in life and in literature.

After it was damaged by fire and later moved, the East Beacon was replaced as a navigational aid by the more inland North Beacon. In 1921, the lighthouse itself was moved to Jeffrey's Hook on the New York side of the Hudson River, where it was overshadowed in 1931 by the bulk of the George Washington Bridge. In 1942, the classic children's book *The Little Red Lighthouse and the Great Gray Bridge*, written by Hildegarde H. Swift and illustrated by Lynd Ward, was published. In this story, the Little Red Lighthouse goes from being proud of its lifesaving function, to being sad that with the lights on the George Washington Bridge above it, it would no longer be necessary. But the Great Gray Bridge calls the lighthouse "Little Brother" and assures it that they both are needed and useful. "Little Red," as the lighthouse became known, was doused in 1947, but was re-lit in a special ceremony in September of 2002, when it was also named a Literary Landmark by the Friends of Libraries U.S.A. So although it is a New York Lighthouse now, "Little Red" can be proud of its New Jersey roots!

In 1822, French physicist Augustin Fresnel invented a large, beehive-shaped glass lens that would forever change the way lighthouse lamps were lit. The thick glass prisms refracted the light from a single lamp, making that light much more powerful and increasing the range of its visibility. Sandy Hook was scheduled to be the first lighthouse in the United States to use the new invention, but when the lens arrived in 1840, workers realized that it was too big for the available space. That 1st order lens, along with a 2nd order lens, was sent over to the more spacious Navesink Light Station in Highlands. Sandy Hook got its Fresnel lens in place in 1857. And in 1889, it was the site of early experiments with electricity.

The Little Red Lighthouse as it stands today.

Growing up around the lighthouse was Fort Hancock, which was established in 1895 and used as a base of military operations until 1974. Starting out as a pair of gun batteries, Fort Hancock ultimately housed more than 10,000 personnel. Many of the early buildings still stand, and these days they are home to a military museum, History House, and some local college and charitable companies. All are worth a look, and the view of New York from the ground in front of "Officer's Row" is breathtaking. In fact, the drive out to the tip of the Hook where the lighthouse stands is worthwhile, even if none of the buildings are open. It is a beautiful trip.

Sandy Hook Lighthouse has tours with talks presented by members of the New Jersey Lighthouse Society. Operating hours vary according to the season, so be sure to check about times before you drive there, but the lighthouse is generally open on weekends from April to mid-December.

A long circular stairway leads through the thick, brick-lined walls, and you can see the Fresnel lens once you reach the top of the tower. This is an average climb of 95 steps, plus a 9-rung ladder to the lantern room. Group size is limited by available space at the top; visitors cannot go out onto the open deck of the tower. The view is outstanding. All the remaining buildings of Fort Hancock, the Verrazano-Narrows Bridge, and of course, New York City are all visible from the tower. While you are at the top, check out the little decorative griffin or dragon figures. They cover the openings of the waterspouts that transport rain run-off from the roof. These spout covers are a very whimsical detail on what is otherwise a simply-styled building.

CHAPTER 3
Navesink Light Station, the Twin Lights

Courtesy of Elinor Veit

Navesink Light Station, the Twin Lights
Lighthouse Road
Highlands, New Jersey, 07732
732-872-1814
www.twin-lights.org

Just down the road from its northerly neighbor, the Sandy Hook Lighthouse, the Twin Lights of Navesink take a different architectural tack altogether. One of the practical attributes of lighthouse design has to be height: the taller the tower, the farther the light can be seen by passing vessels. But for the Twin Lights, site dictated style. Because the land chosen for building the original lights in 1828 was already more than 150 feet above sea level, the towers did not need to be very tall. So two identical octagonal towers were built of blue split stone, standing 320 feet apart and approximately 73 feet tall. They were not originally built with the connecting building that is part of the current layout. "Twin Lights" referred both to their appearance and the fact that having two lights lit at the same time helped to differentiate their light from that of any nearby lighthouses. Navesink is not the only set of "twins" in the United States; more are located in the Northeast.

Not a great deal of thought was put into either the design or the construction of the original two towers. Less than fifteen years after they were built, reports of their poor condition were already in circulation. Despite their flawed appearance however, in 1841, the Navesink Light Station received the first Fresnel lenses used in a United States lighthouse, a 1st order lens in the south tower (theoretically the one that would not fit into the tower at Sandy Hook), a 2nd order lens in the north. Twin Lights was now the brightest lighthouse in the country.

In 1862, the current fortress-style lighthouse was built. It consisted of two towers, now 250 feet apart, and a connecting building that served as storage and living quarters for the keepers and their families. The towers were no longer identical twins – one was square, the other octagonal. The complex was designed by Joseph Lederle, who apparently made the towers different on purpose, though no one seems to be quite sure what that purpose was. The new building was made of brownstone, not the blue stone used to build the original towers. This was an unusual choice, as brownstone had up to this time been used primarily for building housing. Lederle's choice of materials could have been influenced by his design, as the living quarters were a primary part of his plan. And of course, the other big difference in this construction was its quality. Although the original two towers began to deteriorate almost as soon as they were completed, their well-built successors still stand. The North tower had a focal plane of 246 feet, and was upgraded with a 1st order Fresnel lens when the new building was lit.

23

The next historic first for Twin Lights was the switch from whale oil to kerosene (then called mineral oil) in 1883 in the North Tower. That was a huge improvement for the quality of light, and the quality of life for the keepers, because kerosene lamps were much easier to maintain. In 1898, another improvement in lighting came about, with Navesink now being powered by electricity, which was generated on the property in a separate building. While Sandy Hook experimented with electric lighting a bit earlier, Navesink had the first permanent electrical system in place. When the South Tower was electrified, the light in the North Tower was discontinued. The South Tower light was deactivated in 1949, and in 1952 the property was turned over to the Borough of Highlands. The State of New Jersey acquired the property in 1962, and the North Tower was re-lit with a nineteenth-century 5th order Fresnel lens. It remains lit today as a private aid to navigation.

Twin Lights was also home to a first in the field of telegraphy. In 1899, Guglielmo Marconi installed an antenna and receiver at the lighthouse to report the progress of the America's Cup yacht races to waiting reporters at the *New York Herald* newspaper. This worked out so well that Marconi made the installation permanent, making Navesink Lighthouse the first wireless telegraph station in the country.

Today, Navesink Light Station is home to a museum with wonderful exhibits of lighthouse life and historical lifesaving techniques. Visitors can climb the 65 steps that lead to the top of North Tower. The last 10 steps, as well as the lantern room, are closed to the public. It is an easy climb up a circular staircase, and the view of New York Harbor is terrific. While you are there, take some time to explore the museum; there are some very interesting displays there that you will not see anywhere else, and an interesting display about Fresnel lenses. Navesink is open year 'round, but hours vary seasonally, so check before you go.

CHAPTER 4

Sea Girt Lighthouse

Sea Girt Lighthouse
Beacon Boulevard and the Ocean
Sea Girt, New Jersey
732-974-0514

Forty-five miles of ocean separated the lighthouses of Barnegat and
Navesink, too wide a stretch for ships to navigate safely. The Sea Girt Lighthouse was built to bridge that gap. Funding to build the lighthouse was
approved by the United States Congress in 1889, but the land was not
purchased until 1895, and actual construction did not begin until 1896.

The Sea Girt coastal area was originally called Wreck Pond. The name
came from the large number of shipwrecks in the dangerous waters near
the Squan (later Manasquan) Inlet. In fact, one reason for the long delay
from funding to construction was the difficulty in choosing a site. Land
near the inlet's mouth was selected at first, but later the site on Sea Girt
Beach was deemed more advisable. The Squan Inlet Lighthouse name stuck
for a while, but was changed to the Sea Girt Lighthouse in 1897. During
this construction delay alone, it is estimated that more than ninety vessels
met their untimely demise along this small stretch of the coast.

Sea Girt Lighthouse's architecture mirrored the Victorian style of other local properties, and the lighthouse was designed with a 44 foot light tower attached to a house that supplied the living quarters to the lighthouse keeper and his family. This beautiful brick building was the last live-in lighthouse constructed in the United States. Sea Girt's 4th order Fresnel lens was first lit on December 10, 1896, and showed a red flash every fifteen seconds until 1901, when the light color was changed to white. It had a focal plane of 60 feet and was converted to electricity in 1915.

The lighthouse was threatened by water damage soon after it was built, first from the inlet and later from the sea. As early as 1900, fences were built around the property to keep sand from drifting onto the lawn. By the 1920s, the ocean was eroding the foundation, but major damage was averted by the construction of steel pilings along the seaward side of the lighthouse.

Sea Girt, like several other New Jersey lighthouses, was home to a few notable firsts. Harriet Yates became the acting lighthouse keeper in 1910 after the death of her husband, official keeper Abram Yates. Harriet kept the light lit for two months until she was relieved, making her the first woman in America to run a lighthouse. In 1921, Sea Girt was the first lighthouse to use a radio beacon as a navigational aid. Sea Girt Lighthouse, the Ambrose Lightship, and the Fire Island Lightship sent radio signals out to sea. In the same way that lighthouse light characteristics are distinct to avoid confusion, each of these three radio signals was different, enabling the listening ship to easily identify the signal's point of origin. Passing ships used all three signals to triangulate their position by plotting each signal's direction on a chart, knowing that their location was where the three signals intersected. This enabled ships to keep on course, even in weather with low visibility. The Coast Guard took over the lighthouse in 1936.

During World War II, the light at Sea Girt was doused, so it could not be used as an aid to enemy boats, although the radio beacon was active until 1952. Finally decommissioned in the 1950s, the lighthouse was sold to the town of Sea Girt in 1956. The building was used as a meeting place for various local groups until it fell into disrepair. In 1980, town officials had to decide whether to raze the building and sell the property or to raise funds to pay for an extensive renovation. Local residents formed The Sea Girt Lighthouse Citizens Committee Inc., and began the process of raising funds and organizing labor to restore the wonderful old building.

Although the lighthouse has limited operating hours for tours (check before you go), it has become a focal point of the community, hosting classroom tours and meetings of local artists and civic groups. Exhibits in the lighthouse include period furnishings, historic maps, and lighthouse memorabilia. Sea Girt is an easy climb with a total of 42 steps. The first 33 belong to a regular staircase, then there is a 9-rung ladder to the top.

CHAPTER 5
Barnegat Lighthouse

Barnegat Lighthouse
Barnegat Lighthouse State Park
P.O. Box 167
Barnegat Light, NJ 08006
609-494-2016

Located on the northern tip of Long Beach Island, approximately 45 miles south of Sandy Hook, the Barnegat Lighthouse was meant to serve both as a marker of the inlet over which it stood guard and as a marker of coastal hazards to ocean-going vessels. Construction of the first lighthouse, which was designed by Winslow Lewis, began in 1834. First lit in 1835, the tower, which reached a mere 40 feet, was originally fitted with 14-inch reflectors for eleven lamps. In 1851, the Lighthouse Board claimed it was equivalent to a 5th order Fresnel lens and was therefore bright enough for seamen to depend on. But "Old Barney" had a terrible reputation among mariners. They complained that the light was useful only in clear weather, and that if it was hazy or foggy, captains could not tell if it was a light-house or just another sea-going vessel.

Geographically, the lighthouse site is in an important spot, located near the fortieth parallel. The fortieth parallel is a well-traveled part of a prime route for trans-Atlantic sailing. A better, brighter light would be useful to ships making for New York Harbor both from the south and from Europe. In 1854, the Lighthouse received a 4th order Fresnel lens, and in 1855, the board sent Lt. George G. Meade to look at the tower and make recommendations about its future.

Meade was an 1835 graduate of the United States Military Academy at West Point, who would go on to serve in the Union Army during the Civil War, most notably at Gettysburg. Meade was an engineer who had been working for the Lighthouse Board as a supervising engineer and was one of three engineers who oversaw the construction of the Absecon Light-house. He recommended that the Lighthouse Board build a new tower along Absecon's lines, 900 feet south of the existing Barnegat Light. He got there in good time, as the first tower had fallen into the sea by the time construction started on the new tower in 1857. Its light was transferred temporarily to the top of a wooden tower until the new building was com-pleted.

The Barnegat Lighthouse that stands today was first lit with a 1st order Fresnel lens in 1859. The simple, round tower was 165 feet tall and its daymark consisted of a wide red band over a wide white band. The light itself flashed white. That brilliant Fresnel lens stayed atop Barnegat until 1927, when the creation of the Barnegat Lightship 8 miles offshore rendered it obsolete. A smaller beacon stayed lit on the tower until 1944, when the Coast Guard deemed it no longer necessary for navigational purposes. The Fresnel lens was stored for a while at the central lighthouse depot in Staten Island, but was returned to the town of Barnegat in 1954 and is now visible in the Barnegat Light Historical Museum.

Although the new site was much farther from the sea than the previous one, the ocean still tried to claim the tower. By 1869, nine stone jetties had been built to prevent erosion beneath the lighthouse. The jetties prevented the Barnegat tower from going the way of so many other shorefront landmarks. In 1927, ownership of the lighthouse was transferred to the State of New Jersey, and the tower is now the focal point of Barnegat Light State Park. Closed in 1988 for repairs, "Old Barney" has been reopened to the public since 1991.

The operating hours of Barnegat Lighthouse vary seasonally, so visitors should check before going. The climb to the top is more difficult than average, with a circular staircase of 217 steps, but the view is well worth the effort. While on a visit to the lighthouse, be sure and stop by the Barnegat Light Historical Museum to see the Fresnel lens and other displays of local history.

CHAPTER 6

Tucker's Island Lighthouse

Tucker's Island Lighthouse at the Tuckerton Seaport
120 West Main Street
P.O. Box 52
Tuckerton, NJ 08087
609-296-8868
www.TuckertonSeaport.org

   The story surrounding the Tucker's Island Lighthouse reads like a ro-
mance or mystery novel. Over a period of about 150 years, Tucker's Beach
was transformed from undeveloped wilderness into a fashionable resort
area, then disappeared entirely under the ocean's waves.
   The area first known as Tucker's Beach was part of the old South Beach
landmass until a fierce storm in 1800 carved a new inlet (later named the
Little Egg Harbor Inlet) leading to the Little Egg Harbor and Great Bay of
Mullica. By 1900, shifting sands had brought Tucker's Beach in close contact with the more northern Long Beach land mass, eventually linking one
to the other. In 1920, another great storm whipped through the area, caus-
ing Tucker's Island to separate from Long Beach Island once again. The
ensuing years caused Tucker's Island to grow smaller and smaller, losing

its buildings one by one to the sea, and eventually disappearing altogether by 1952. With the changes brought by time and tide, Tucker's Island is slowly becoming visible again after an absence of more than thirty years.

The area was named Tucker's Beach in honor of Reuben Tucker, who purchased the land in 1745. By 1765, he had established a boarding house, attracting visitors from as far away as Philadelphia. Early guests to this establishment included hunters and fishermen. Tucker supplemented his income by selling supplies and alcohol to his guests and passing seamen.

The first lighthouse on Tucker's Beach was built in 1848 to mark the inlet into Little Egg Harbor. By all accounts it was a dimly lit, one-story brick building. The dazzling light of Absecon, constructed in 1857, made the Tucker's Beach light all but obsolete, and it was discontinued in 1859. However, in 1868 a 4th order Fresnel lens was brought to the Island, and when renovations were complete, the lighthouse was a two-story building with a square black tower on top. The exterior of the lantern room was painted red, and the light had a focal plane of 50 feet. Its light shone a series of six red flashes followed by one white flash, and was visible 12 miles out to sea.

In 1870, hotels and cottages were built in what was then known as Sea Haven. The population of the little island began to swell, with permanent residents joined by guests on summer holiday. In 1872, "The Mary," a small steamboat, began to ferry guests from the mainland town of Tuckerton to hotels such as the Columbia and the St. Albans, and this period became the peak of the little island's prosperity, until changing geography again wreaked its toll.

The same relentless ocean that formed the island continued to pound away. What was once dry land became soggy and waterlogged at high tide. Because there was no other way to get to the resorts from the ferry landing without getting wet, local baymen sometimes worked by carrying the guests to their hotels. The development of train service from the New Jersey mainland to nearby Beach Haven in 1886 hastened the decline of Sea Haven's popularity as a summer destination. The population shrank, hotels were abandoned, and slowly, inexorably, Tucker's Island was washed back into the ocean. In 1925, some of the cottages and abandoned hotels disappeared, and in 1927, the lighthouse was swept into the sea. The last building disappeared from Sea Haven in 1935.

View of Lenape Indian display in the 1st floor of the Lighthouse museum.

The Tuckerton Seaport, located in the town of Tuckerton, is the brainstorm of a group of sportsmen from Southern Ocean County. They began meeting in the late 1980s with the idea of purchasing a site to create a gun club to teach the baymen's art of waterfowling. Their dreams grew bigger however, leading to the founding of the Barnegat Bay Decoy and Baymen's Museum. Ground was broken for the museum in early 1993. But the idea of honoring the baymen and women whose lifestyles and traditions were being lost as the modern age took over grew again. Additional funding from the State of New Jersey in 1994 enabled the purchase of 11 acres on Tuckerton Creek, where the ever-expanding Tuckerton Seaport now stands. Additional purchases have increased the Seaport's holdings to just under forty acres, and there are plans to create additional buildings and exhibits.

Open since May of 2000, the Seaport is home to a beautiful re-creation of the original Tucker's Island Lighthouse. The first two floors are host to museum displays of local history, including the history of the Island itself, and the changes the Island went through over time. Getting up to the top of the tower is an easy climb. There are 40 steps; the first 25 are wide and carpeted (and visitors can stop on the second floor for more exhibits), the last 15 comprise a small circular staircase to the third-story tower room. There is not a light at the top of the tower, but there is a very accessible display with a Fresnel lens on the second floor, and the climb to the top yields a lovely view of the rest of the Seaport and Tuckerton Creek. Not to be missed at the building's entrance is a set of enlarged photos taken in the moments that the Tucker's Island Lighthouse was tumbling into the ocean. While at the Seaport, visitors should also check out the other buildings on the property. There are exhibits of the art of decoy making and boat building, and others that illustrate how the Baymen made their living from the sea and what their lives were like in years past. A visit to Tuckerton Seaport is a great way to spend the day, and has lots of terrific kid-friendly activities.

CHAPTER 7

Absecon Lighthouse

Absecon Lighthouse
31 South Rhode Island Ave.
Atlantic City, NJ 08401
609-449-1360
www.abseconlighthouse.org

As early as the 1840s, local residents, led by Dr. Jonathan Pitney (the 'Father of Atlantic City'), called for a lighthouse on Absecon Beach to warn ships of the dangers of the Absecon and Brigantine Shoals. It took the 1854 wreck of the *Powhattan* to add the needed emphasis to Pitney's request. The *Powhattan* was carrying a large group of emigrant passengers to the United States from Europe. She sank during a terrible storm at sea, and more than 300 crew members and passengers were killed. But construction of Absecon Lighthouse did not begin until 1855. Its 1st order Fresnel lens showed a fixed white light, was powered by mineral oil (kerosene), and was first lit on January 15, 1857. This was another area of the New Jersey coast where ships were regularly lost. To underline the point that Pitney was correct – there were no shipwrecks along Absecon Shoals in the first ten months of the lighthouse's operation.

Although he was not the only engineer to work at the site, the primary supervising engineer was Lt. George G. Meade. Absecon bears strong similarities to its sister light to the North, Barnegat, and its sister light to the South, Cape May. Experts are not sure exactly who designed the plans from which these three lighthouses took their basic structure, and available historical plans do not have signatures on them. The three towers, while similar, are not identical. Meade may have been responsible for altering all three to suit their particular locales and needs. Meade definitely worked on Barnegat Lighthouse, and may very well have been assigned to Cape May. Absecon was the first of these three assignments he undertook for the Lighthouse Board, and here he supervised the construction that was done by a local contractor. As mentioned in other chapters, Meade went on to succeed as a commander in the Union Army during the Civil War.

The original daymark of Absecon Lighthouse was its natural red brick color. It has had several color changes over the years, although some experts disagree about the dates of some of the paint jobs. In 1871, Absecon was painted white with a red central band, and it kept that coloring until 1898, when it was painted orange with a black central band. Perhaps this was to keep sailors from confusing Absecon with the red-over-white Barnegat Lighthouse just up the coast. Sometime before the 1907 Lighthouse Board condition report came out, Absecon's color was changed to yellow with a black central band. In 1948, the color was changed to white with a blue central band. These were the official colors of Atlantic City. Because the lighthouse was decommissioned by this time, and its primary function was as a tourist attraction, it is likely that this color change had more of an aesthetic purpose than a navigational one. In the late 1960s, the lighthouse's daymark was changed back to white with a red central band. In 1998, Absecon Lighthouse's color was restored to yellow with a black central band. This coloration was chosen because it was the last daymark from the period when the lighthouse was actively working as a navigational aid.

By 1876, erosion began to threaten the lighthouse, so stone and wood jetties were built to keep the sand in place. Unlike the jetties at Barnegat, Absecon's jetties have disappeared from view beneath the sand. Interestingly enough, while the lighthouse was originally built a good distance from the shoreline, then threatened by the sea in the 1870s, it now stands two blocks off shore. This is due partly to time and tide, and partly to the effectiveness of the jetties in building up the beach. Absecon was electrified in 1925, and decommissioned in 1933 when an electric beacon on Steel Pier fulfilled its navigational function. In the 1940s, the decaying lighthouse keeper's house was destroyed.

Absecon lighthouse was formally deeded over to Atlantic City in 1946, and twenty years later it was sold to the State of New Jersey. In 1988, the Inlet Public/Private Association was formed as an advocate for redevelopment in the Inlet section of Atlantic City. In 1993, the IPPA adopted Absecon Lighthouse, taking responsibility for raising funds for and overseeing its restoration. In May of 1997, the IPPA began the costly restoration of the lighthouse, including a reproduction of the keeper's house. The new keeper's house was lost to a fire in 1998, but the tower re-opened to the public on schedule in 1999. In October 2001, a new keeper's house made its debut, featuring murals of a lighthouse keeper's life painted by artist Linda Wexler. Now it is host to a museum focused on the history of the lighthouse and its neighborhood, and the grounds play host to a self-guided tour.

At 169 feet, Absecon is the tallest lighthouse in New Jersey, making it a harder climb than most. It has more steps than any of the other New Jersey lighthouses, with 228 steps on the circular staircase, plus 12 more leading up to the lantern room. The original 1st order Fresnel lens is still there, one of the few historical lenses that have never been removed. Visitors to the top are treated to some terrific views, both of the ocean and of Atlantic City proper. Other seafaring attractions in the neighborhood include the Ocean Life Center in Gardner's Basin. The Center has displays of ecology and marine life, including a 750-gallon "touch tank" where visitors can touch some of the local marine life.

43

CHAPTER 8
Hereford Inlet Lighthouse

Hereford Inlet Lighthouse
1st and Central Avenues
North Wildwood, New Jersey 08260
609-522-4520

A lot of marine traffic flowed through Hereford Inlet. The Inlet was used first as a safe haven for ships to prepare their catches for market or to avoid being caught at sea in a storm, and later as a link from the Atlantic Ocean to the Intra-Coastal Waterway. A small beacon was stationed on the south side of the Inlet as early as 1849, but the full-scale lighthouse that is visible today was not commissioned until 1872.

Hereford Inlet Lighthouse was built in what was then known as the fishing village of Anglesea (now North Wildwood), on land that was purchased for $150. The light was first lit in 1874, and the treacherous nature of the area was illustrated almost immediately. Hereford's first lighthouse keeper, John Marche, drowned when his boat capsized less than three months after he had taken up his post. The lighthouse had a 4th order Fresnel lens and showed a fixed white light. Its focal plane measured 53 feet. Under the auspices of keeper Freeling Hewitt, who served for forty-five years (1875-1920), Baptist services were held in the lighthouse until a church was built. The lighthouse remained on its first site until 1913, when the pounding tide, with help from a large storm, finally eroded its foundation. It was moved 150 feet inland to its current location, and that restoration was completed in 1914. The Hereford Lighthouse remained in operation until 1964, when its navigational function was passed over to a more easily maintained automatic marine beacon, which was fitted onto a large iron light tower erected behind the existing lighthouse. After being put to use for a while by the Marine Police, the building was leased to the City of North Wildwood in 1982.

One of the most interesting things about the Hereford Inlet Lighthouse is its design. While most New Jersey lighthouses are simple towers, designed with utility and practicality in mind, the Hereford property is a carefully thought-out testament to the glories of Victorian Stick style, with spacious, well-appointed living quarters for the keeper and his family. At the time, the job of lighthouse keeper was still a rigorous one, but at least the keepers here could return to the comfort of their snug house at night's end.

The Hereford Lighthouse was designed by Paul J. Pelz when he was the chief draftsman of the Lighthouse Board; it is the only Stick style lighthouse standing on the East Coast. It has been compared to the Adams Point Lighthouse in Oregon, the Point Fermin Light in California, and the East Brother Island Light in California (also a Pelz design). Pelz went on to design the Thomas Jefferson Building of the Library of Congress, a project he would oversee until 1892.

In 1982, hundreds of local residents began the painstaking process of raising money and restoring Pelz's building. It reopened to the public in 1983. To the delight of the North Wildwood's many residents and visitors, the ugly light tower was removed in 1986, and its automated beacon was placed in the newly restored lighthouse tower, making the lighthouse useful once again. Also in 1986, extensive work began on what is now considered one of the finest gardens in South Jersey. More than 170 plant varieties and thousands of flowers thrive on a half-acre site that had previously been nothing more than sandy, empty lots. Try to plan your visit when the garden is in bloom, but the lighthouse itself is worth the trip. It is a very well-maintained site and was recently repainted to its earlier straw color.

Hereford is an easy climb – 44 wooden steps broken up by two floors of the house where you can stop and enjoy exhibits of the lighthouse's early history. Be aware that no cameras are allowed inside the building. Any visitor with a camera will be asked to lock it in a car or check it at the front desk. Hereford Lighthouse is once again a bright spot in the community, home to many activities throughout the year, including craft shows, art exhibits, and the town's annual Christmas celebration.

Hereford Gardens. *Courtesy of Bill Volpe*

CHAPTER 9
Cape May Lighthouse

Cape May Lighthouse
Lighthouse Road
Cape May Point, NJ 08212

Contact info: Mid-Atlantic Center for the Arts
1048 Washington Street, P.O. Box 340
Cape May, NJ 08204-0340
609-884-5404
800-275-4278
www.capemaymac.org (Click the lighthouse link)

As with other lighthouses on New Jersey's coast, the Cape May light-house at Cape May Point is not the first such structure to have been built there. The first documented lighthouse on the Point was built in 1822 and first lit in 1823. It was a 70 foot tall brick tower with a flashing light. Its site was too near the waterline, and by 1847, the tower was waterlogged at high tide, so it was decommissioned, soon to topple into the ocean. A second tower was built about a third of a mile inland. It was made of brick like the first tower, but was taller. The second tower was lit from 1847 to 1859. The foundation and bottom 10 feet of the second tower were used as a small building for various purposes for the rest of the 1800s, but ulti-mately the building disappeared into the waves like the first tower.

The site chosen for the third lighthouse tower was an additional 1,000 feet inland. After the tower was built, two keepers' houses were added, one of which is now used by Cape May Point State Park. In 1902, one of the keeper's houses was expanded to comfortably house three keepers and their families. The building that houses the gift shop and the admissions desk was built in 1893 for use as an oil house.

Cape May Lighthouse was electrified in 1938, and then doused in 1941, as were many of the other coastal lights at the start of WWII. Its 1st order Fresnel lens was removed in 1946, and is now on display in the Cape May County Museum, in the town of Cape May Courthouse. A modern DCB-36 lens replaced the Fresnel lens, and the light was relit. After fifty-six years of service, the DCB-36 was retired on November 11, 2002, and a new DCB-224 took its place. Shining brightly, the light of the new beacon can be seen up to 24 miles away, its visibility limited only by the curvature of the earth. The light remains lit today, under management of the Coast Guard, while the tower itself is leased to the Mid-Atlantic Center for the Arts, also known as MAC.

Cape May Lighthouse bears a strong resemblance to the Absecon and Barnegat Lighthouses; experts believe it may have been another project by George G. Meade, but that connot be proven by existing documentation. The tower measures 157 feet and 6 inches to the top, with a focal plane of 175 feet, and a solid white daymark. Cape May showed a flashing light to differentiate it from its neighbors to the north. One of the big problems at Cape May Point was the wind – there were reports in 1875 of wind that rattled the lighthouse so much that oil spilled out of the lamps. To fight the wind, the Cape May Lighthouse was built with two concentric walls for added strength. The outer wall is well over 3 feet thick at the base, where the inner wall measures 8.5 inches, and there is a space between the two. This tower is not going easily into the sea like its two predecessors!

Cape May Lighthouse has always been a point of interest for tourists. The tall gleaming structure, which provides outstanding views of the sea, has been a must-see for vacationers throughout the years. Today it hosts thousands of visitors each summer, in part because of the wonderful restoration job overseen by MAC, which also supervises other historic properties and events in Cape May.

Nearly $2 million has been spent restoring the Lighthouse and its environs, and it shows; it is a beautiful place to spend an afternoon. Cape May Lighthouse is open year 'round, but hours vary seasonally, so check before you go.

Just down Sunset Boulevard from the Lighthouse is Sunset Beach, another must-see destination, especially at sunset. This beach is the southernmost tip of New Jersey – the view is gorgeous any time of day, but at sunset Nature really pulls out all the stops with a wide display of color. Every evening when the American flag is taken down from its pole, a recording of "God Bless America" is played, and hundreds of people come out to take in the sunset. Look on the beach for Cape May Diamonds (a local quartz), and check out the remains of the Atlantus, a ship made of concrete that ran aground here in 1926 and has been slowly disappearing ever since. While in the area, take time to visit Cape May, which offers a treasure trove of Victorian architecture, with many shops, restaurants, and family activities to enjoy.

CHAPTER 10
East Point Lighthouse

East Point Lighthouse
Lighthouse Road
Maurice Township, NJ

For more information contact
Maurice River Historical Society
210 North High Street
Millville, NJ 08332
856-327-3714

Situated at the mouth of the Maurice River, the East Point Lighthouse (known until 1913 as the Maurice River Lighthouse), is a beautiful testament to the isolated life a lighthouse keeper often lived.

Built in 1849 of whitewashed brick, the tower protrudes from the center of a two-story keeper's house. East Point is the last standing lighthouse on the New Jersey side of the Delaware Bay, and the second oldest standing lighthouse in New Jersey (second only to Sandy Hook). It housed a 6th order Fresnel lens from 1852 until WWII caused it to be extinguished in 1941.

East Point showed a fixed white light, had a focal plane of 43 feet and was automated in 1911. The lighthouse was re-lit by the U.S. Coast Guard in 1980 using a 250 millimeter modern lens.

Deeded over to the Division of Fish, Game, and Wildlife in 1956, the vacant building sustained continual damage from weather and vandals. In 1971, the same year a devastating fire set by a trespasser did extensive damage to the building, a group of concerned local citizens formed the Maurice River Historical Society in order to save the lighthouse. The property is still undergoing renovations. East Point has very limited operating hours, so visitors should call for more information. It is an easy climb, with regular house steps to the second story, followed by a short circular staircase to the tower top. But even if you can't get inside, there is something very appealing about the little brick lighthouse on the salt marsh, and it is definitely worth a trip.

CHAPTER 11

Finn's Point Rear Range Light

Finn's Point Rear Range Light
Contact info:
Supawna Meadows National Wildlife Refuge
197 Lighthouse Road
Pennsville, NJ 08070
856-935-1487

Part of a range of lights built to help ships navigate the Delaware Bay, Finn's Point Rear Range Light was built in 1876. The iron structure was originally constructed in Buffalo, New York, by the Kellogg Bridge Company. It was sent in sections by rail to Salem, New Jersey, then transported to its current spot by a mule cart, and assembled on site.

Other buildings originally in this area included the front range light (destroyed in the 1930s), a keeper's house, and an oil house. All of those are gone now, although there are a few bricks in the ground to mark where the oil house once stood. The 115-foot tall tower was first lit in 1877, showing a double-fixed white light in a 5th order Fresnel lens. Its focal plane measures 105 feet, and the light was automated in 1934. Finn's Point became obsolete in 1950 when the Delaware River channel was enlarged. Abandoned, the lighthouse fell into disrepair, and in 1977, the keeper's house was demolished after vandalism and fire made it too unsteady to be repaired. In the 1970s, a citizen's group called the Save the Lighthouse Committee was formed, and the lighthouse was restored in 1983.

Finn's Point is an average climb of 130 steps, 119 of which are on a circular iron staircase. The last 11 steps are wooden ladder rungs up to the lantern room. The circular staircase is enclosed in a black metal housing, and it can get very hot in the summer. There is a 5th order Fresnel lens on display, although officials are not sure if it is the light's original lens. Hours for climbing the lighthouse are limited, but because the tower stands in the Supawna Meadows National Wildlife Refuge, you can walk up to the tower to take photographs or just to see it any day of the week. Visitors to Supawna can also take advantage of the many nature trails available to hike or stroll – this is a very pretty area in which to look for local flora and fauna.

CHAPTER 12
Tinicum Rear Range Light

Tinicum Rear Range Light
2nd and Mantua
Paulsboro, NJ 08066
856-423-1505

Built in 1880, the Tinicum Rear Range Light is part of a set of range lights constructed to help ships navigate the Delaware Bay. Tinicum is still active on the Delaware, and currently shows a fixed red light.

Other buildings constructed in the nineteenth century for the keeper included a living quarters, an oil house, a chicken coop, and a privy, although none of these are standing today. Originally fitted with a parabolic reflector, the focal plane of Tinicum is 83 feet, and it was automated in 1967.

Tinicum has limited hours when it is open for visitors, so call in advance, but it can be climbed. The tower is 112 feet tall and has a 112 step circular staircase to the top. The climb is rated as average, but in extremely hot weather the enclosed staircase can get a little toasty. Three windows that open were installed in 2003 to help cool the staircase, so if you have climbed it in the past, conditions have definitely improved.

About the New Jersey Lighthouse Society

The New Jersey Lighthouse Society is a non-profit association dedicated to educating the public about and preserving lighthouses in New Jersey and the United States. The group of about one thousand members meets four times each year at sites around the state. The Society also sponsors lighthouse tours throughout the East Coast. Members are deeply involved in guiding tours at Sandy Hook and Absecon Lighthouses.

A popular annual autumn event is the New Jersey Lighthouse Challenge. On two days each October, all eleven lighthouses are open to the public for tours. Each participating site has its own souvenir to commemorate your visit, and you must visit each site to collect them all. Challenge participants may begin at any of the lighthouses and follow the shoreline in either direction. Lighthouse Society members will be at each site to greet guests. Visit one, several, or all eleven for a fun family weekend!

For more information please contact:
New Jersey Lighthouse Society
P.O. Box 332
Navesink, NJ 07752-0332
856-546-0514
www.njlhs.burlco.org
NJLHS@burlco.org

Bibliography

Gately, Bill. *Sentinels of the Shore A Guide to Lighthouses and Lightships of New Jersey*. Harvey Cedars, New Jersey: Down the Shore Publishing, 1998.

Heap, D. P. *Ancient and Modern Lighthouses*. Boston, Massachusetts: Ticknor and Company, 1889.

Holland, F. Ross. *America's Lighthouses; Their Illustrated History Since 1716*. Brattleboro, Vermont: S. Greene Press, 1972.

Jordan, Joe J. *Cape May Point The Illustrated History: 1875 to the Present*. Atglen, Pennsylvania: Schiffer Publishing Ltd., 2003.

Mountford, Kent. *Closed Sea: From the Manasquan to the Mullica, a History of Barnegat Bay*. Harvey Cedars, New Jersey: Down the Shore Publishing, 2002.

Smith, Samuel Stelle. *Sandy Hook and the Land of the Navesink*. Monmouth Beach, New Jersey: Philip Freneau Press, 1963.

Stevenson, Thomas. *Lighthouse Construction and Illumination*. London, New York: E. & F. N. Spon, 1881.

Veasey, David, *Guarding New Jersey's Shore Lighthouses and Life-Saving Stations*. Charleston, South Carolina: Arcadia Publishing, 2000.